# Anyone Can Paint—*I Promise*

# Anyone Can Paint—*I Promise*

**Robert H. Garden**

Photographs by Jack Dannels

DAVID McKAY COMPANY, INC. · NEW YORK

Library of Congress Cataloging in Publication Data

Garden, Robert H.
    Anyone can paint—I promise

    SUMMARY: A teaching method designed to get the student painting quickly and easily. Includes information on equipment, various techniques, and step-by-step instructions for painting sea- and landscapes, a snow-capped mountain, and a still life.
    1. Painting—Technique—Juvenile literature.
(1. Painting—Technique)  I. Dannels, Jack.  II. Title.
ND1146.G37     751.4'5     76-13272
ISBN 0-679-20323-0

Manufactured in the United States of America

# CONTENTS

# Anyone Can Paint—*I Promise*

Because of a fascination with the beauty of nature, I determined at a very early age to become an artist. Since I lived in a very rural area of the United States, art instruction and art supplies were not readily available. As a matter of fact, I was unaware that such things even existed. So, at the age of seven, I began to experiment with materials at hand, creating my own paints using mud, flower petals, berries, food coloring, and linseed oil. As for brushes, hair from the tails of my dog and cat served quite satisfactorily for a while. (Cat hair, by the way, is a good deal softer than dog hair.)

My experiments continued until my parents, both of whom worked and were unaware of my dabblings, discovered what was going on. Fortunately for me, they were so impressed with what I had accomplished that they went out immediately to buy canvases and oil paints. My career zoomed! I sold my first painting when I was eight years old, receiving eighty dollars for it—and not to a relative, either.

I had my first formal art training during my first year in college, and my first insight into the shortcomings of many instructors: Many instructors were really disinterested in what the students learned. I began to realize the necessity for a well-planned program when instructing beginners, and especially students who took their art seriously. I realized that the teaching and the learning could be done in much less time than was being used. Actually, I put myself in the teacher's place and asked myself: What can I do to accelerate the students' progress?

In the fast-moving lives of today, people do not desire or expect to waste their time with long-drawn-out procedures that are completely unnecessary. So, I developed a method of teaching that eliminates a lot of the unnecessary trial and error of older methods. Students learn quickly and easily, and derive much satisfaction from immediate results.

My ultimate goal is to make painting so simple that anyone with the desire to paint can do so. In my opinion, anyone with the desire to paint automatically has the talent—talent that only needs to be developed. That is why I have simplified my teaching techniques to the point that a logical sequence of events can be demonstrated. A refinement of details may be added as one progresses. For instance, to spend hour after hour learning the elements of perspective is unnecessary when one is just beginning, but can become very important as one develops a facility for painting. I have just put my teaching techniques in their proper perspective.

If you are a beginner just learning to paint, I hope this book will make the learning so easy that you will go on to develop your ability to its fullest extent, and that you enjoy every minute of it.

## ESSENTIAL

12 × 16 disposable palette

oil cups

turpentine

linseed oil (optional)

retouch varnish (liquid only)

#3 trowel-shaped painting knife

#12 flat bristle brush

#7 flat bristle brush

#5 round sable brush

#6 script liner

#6 bristle fan blender

smock or apron

easel

16 × 20 canvas board or stretched canvas
or 18 × 24 canvas board or stretched canvas

## HELPFUL ADDITIONS

TV table

roll of paper towels

pad and pencil

"quickie" hand cleaner

Titanium White ✓
Cadmium Yellow Light ✓
Cadmium Red Light ✓
Cadmium Orange ✓
Burnt Sienna ✓
Yellow Ochre ✓
Raw Sienna ✓
Burnt Umber ✓
Ultramarine Blue ✓
Raw Umber ✓
Viridian Green ✓
Alizarin Crimson ✓
Prussian Blue —

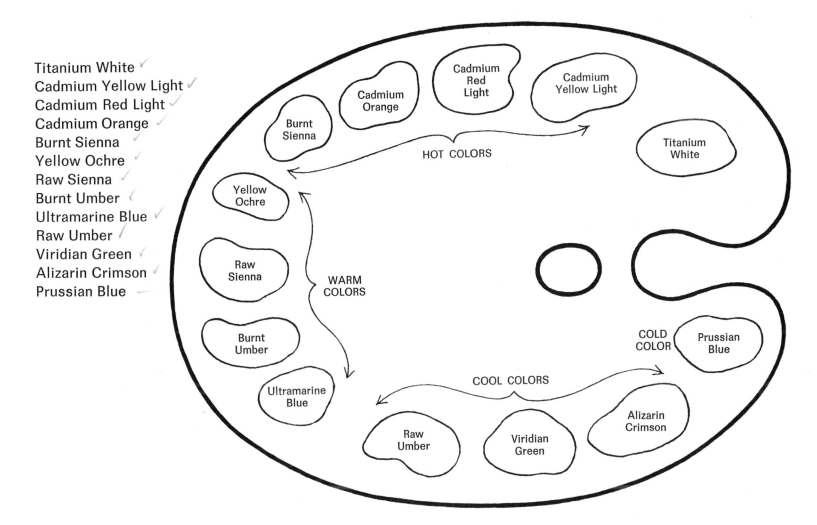

**The Palette**

The palette was designed with you, the student, in mind. Most students who are just beginning to paint are hesitant about investing a lot of money in unnecessary materials and equipment. For that reason, I have not included any paints that you do not need.

This palette is complete with six transparent colors, six opaque colors, and one white (which is opaque). I'm assuming, of course, that you know the difference between opaque and transparent. It is no different with oils. You can see through the transparent colors, but the opaque colors cover so that you cannot see through them. Transparent colors are used to produce shadows, which are transparent. You can see into them. You can be standing in a shadow and still see the details within it. Transparent colors are also used when painting glass or other objects, such as a green bottle, that you can see through. To get a transparent effect, you naturally use a transparent color.

The palette (see page 3) is laid out starting with Titanium White, which is neutral; it is neither a warm nor a cool color. It continues from the hot colors (Cadmium Yellow Light, Cadmium Red Light, Cadmium Orange, and Burnt Sienna) to the warm colors (Yellow Ochre, Raw Sienna, Burnt Umber, and Ultramarine Blue) to the cool colors (Raw Umber, Viridian Green, and Alizarin Crimson) to the cold (Prussian Blue).

I did not choose these colors because I personally like all of them; the palette has a precise reason for its arrangement. There are very precise reasons for the use of warm and cool and hot colors that are related to the physiological response of the human eye to light reflected from those colors.

Technically speaking, the human eye can see only those colors ranging in wave length from 400 to 800 millimicrons. *(A millimicron—1000th part of a micron, or 1,000,000th part of a millimeter—is the unit used to measure the length of a light wave.)* Colors in the range of the shorter wave lengths (400 millimicrons) are the cool colors; those with the longer wave lengths (800 millimicrons) are the hot colors. The eye has a tendency to see the hot colors first, followed by perception of the cool colors. There are wave lengths of color above and below the visible range, but the human eye is unable to distinguish them; they include the infrared and ultraviolet.

The importance of cool and warm colors is in the effects they produce on a canvas. Cool colors seem to recede, giving the effect of depth, whereas warm colors seem to come forward. This is the reason one can make objects painted on a flat surface appear far in the distance. That is why the use of cool colors is stressed when distance is the objective.

Using White does not achieve the effect of depth; it only changes the tint of the color. Adding Black, which is also neutral, changes the shade of a color. So, to achieve the effect of depth, one may add White to lighten the color but must also use a cool color to create depth. Colors should get cooler and lighter as they recede and warmer and darker as they come forward.

For your convenience, the palette is arranged with the colors ranging from cold to cool to warm to hot. There are three basic colors among the transparent colors, as well as among the opaque.

The colors we see are the results of the interaction of light and the surface from which it is reflected. For instance, a beam of white light is made up of colors ranging in wave length from about 400 millimicrons (violet) to about 800 milli-microns (red). The complete range includes a series of colors: red, orange, yellow, green, blue, indigo, and violet, in that order. When a beam of light passes through a prism, its rays are refracted in such a way that a spectrum of colors appears. You see the same effect when light passing through raindrops forms a rainbow, or when you look at a diamond. Experimenting, man has been able to produce pigments that duplicate the colors of the spectrum by the way in which light is either reflected or absorbed when it strikes a surface.

Keep in mind that white light is composed of colors of light; when you look at a color such as Cadmium Yellow Light, all of the colors of light are absorbed with the exception of yellow, which is reflected. If you see a white object or white surface, then all of the colors are being reflected. A black surface absorbs all of the colors; there is an absence of color. If it sounds complicated, don't fret about it. Someone else has done the work of producing pigments that serve your purpose.

When you look at the palette, you might think that there are relatively few colors on it, and only one green. Correction! There are many greens, and many other colors as well, even though you see only twelve colors on the palette. Let's take green, for instance. We have Viridian Green, which is seldom used in painting green objects such as bushes, trees, grass, etc. It is used mainly for transparent objects—glass, water, shadows, and the like—or for creating the illusion of depth in the sky.

Experiment with the palette. Try to make different greens by mixing Prussian Blue with Viridian Green, or with Raw Umber or Burnt Umber or Raw Sienna or Yellow Ochre or Burnt Sienna or Cadmium Orange or Cadmium Red Light or Cadmium Yellow Light.

You can see from the above that we have only scratched the surface. Try the same combinations using Ultramarine Blue rather than Prussian Blue, or try mixing Prussian Blue with Ultramarine Blue plus each of the previously mentioned colors. Is this not enough? Then try Prussian Blue plus Ultramarine Blue plus Viridian Green plus each of the other colors. Perhaps you might try Cadmium Yellow Light plus Yellow Ochre plus Raw Sienna plus Prussian or Ultramarine Blue or Viridian Green. In other words, the number of greens one can achieve is endless. Viridian Green plus Alizarin Crimson will also make green. It will also make a violet or a blue.

You could use Ultramarine Blue plus Burnt Umber (which

are the colors I use for achieving black) with Cadmium Yellow Light to make a green. Raw Umber plus Cadmium Yellow Light will also make a green. You have many possibilities.

Black is considered a warm color. Ivory Black is made from charred animal bones mixed with linseed oil. When used with other colors, it tends to make them appear muddy or dirty—quite naturally, because charcoal smears and gives the appearance of being dirty. That is why I use Burnt Umber plus Ultramarine Blue to make black. It does not make the colors appear muddy but is still a warm color, just as Ivory Black is.

Orange is an interesting color also. It can be made by mixing Alizarin Crimson with Raw Sienna, or with Yellow Ochre or Cadmium Orange or Cadmium Yellow Light. For burnt orange mix Burnt Umber with Cadmium Red Light, or with Cadmium Orange or Burnt Sienna; use Burnt Sienna or even Burnt Umber by itself. There are other mixtures, such as Yellow Ochre plus Raw Sienna plus Alizarin Crimson plus Cadmium Red Light, and Yellow Ochre plus Raw Sienna plus Cadmium Orange plus Alizarin Crimson.

Violet can be made with Prussian Blue plus Alizarin Crimson; Prussian Blue plus Cadmium Red Light plus Alizarin Crimson; Ultramarine Blue plus Alizarin Crimson; Ultramarine Blue plus Prussian Blue plus Alizarin Crimson plus Cadmium Red Light; Viridian Green plus Alizarin Crimson; and other combinations.

Red is made with Alizarin Crimson plus Cadmium Red Light.

To paint an object the color of burnt sienna in the foreground, you would use Burnt Sienna; but, if you were to paint the same object into the background, you could use Raw Sienna plus Alizarin Crimson, which makes a burnt sienna color that is cool and thus recedes.

Alizarin Crimson is a strange color. It makes reds yet is not itself considered a red. If you mix white with it you get a pink, but one that cannot be used for any particular object. A flower, perhaps, would be the only possibility.

When we speak about a colored object, we are not talking about one color but of five different values. Look at a blob of color squeezed out of the tube—yellow, for instance. If you were to try to paint that blob of yellow onto a canvas to look like the blob as it rests on a surface, you would have to use at least five different values of yellow. Where the color is facing the light, you would use the actual color of the object or Value #1, the *body tone*. As the color goes away from the light, it should change to Value #2, the *body shadow*. Value #3 is the *cast shadow*. If the blob of paint is resting on a green surface, then the green will cause Value #4, *reflected light*. The brightest light you see on top closest to the light source is Value #5, *highlight*. Each value in itself, such as the highlight, has nine different values, but if you concern yourself with the five basic ones at first, you will automatically achieve several of the nine values.

Let's look at the combinations that achieve each value for that same yellow. Body tone (#1) is easy: Just use yellow. Body shadow (#2) is achieved by using the color *opposite* to that of yellow, which is violet. You would add a little violet to make the body shadow. To make the cast shadow (Value #3) —the shadow of yellow—simply use more violet with the yellow. To get reflected light (#4), use a little of the color of the surface on which the blob rests; in this case, green. To make the highlight (#5), resort back to the opposite color, violet, with lots of white. This will achieve the best highlight and is considered a complementary color.

The above technique works fine for everything except metals and metal objects. The reason it does not work for metal objects is that metal consists of the reflections of everything around it, with the exception of a slight color change imparted by gold, brass, silver, copper, et cetera. Each metal has its own color, and in many different values, so this has to be taken into consideration.

The three primary colors are red, yellow, and blue. Related to the palette, Cadmium Yellow is the primary yellow; Ultramarine Blue is the primary blue; and Alizarin Crimson plus Cadmium Red Light is the primary red. The secondary colors are violet, orange, and green, and are produced by mixtures of the primary colors: blue and red to make violet, blue and yellow to make green, red and yellow to make orange. Then, of course, there are many intermediate colors that may be achieved by mixtures of colors that are adjacent to each other on the color wheel. For instance, yellow plus orange to make yellow-orange, yellow and green to make yellow-green, red and violet to make red-violet, red and orange to make red-orange, blue and violet to make blue-violet, and blue plus green to make blue-green.

Sunlight and incandescent lights, such as a light bulb or the flame of a burning candle, contain all the spectrum colors, or perhaps I should say the whole range of visible light rays, those between 400 and 800 millimicrons. The hotter light sources contain more blue than the cooler ones. For instance, candlelight appears yellow compared to sunlight. When a primary color—yellow, for example—is eliminated from white light, the remaining combinations of color will appear as the complementary color, in this case violet.

You may ask what all this has to do with painting, but it helps to know these things when you start to paint. It makes you more observant of the interplay of color in the things you are about to paint. To paint a flame, such as a candle or a fire burning under a metal pot, could be most correctly achieved by first knowing what color the flame appears to be when it comes into contact with a certain metal surface. Or what gases are released from the paraffin of the candle.

The flame of a candle is complicated. If you observe it closely, you will find four different bands of color. The elliptical shape around the wick is darker than the color next to it. This is a soft orange. The second band produces all of the light put out by the candle; it is a yellow color. Around the outside of the second band is a third band. It is a very faint blue, and the fourth band is a little brighter blue at the base of the wick, shaped like a deep dish.

A candle is a mixture of two solids, both of which are white. The two are paraffin and stearic acid, consisting mostly of carbon and hydrogen. The melting process creates gases. The first band consists of various compounds of carbon and hydrogen. As it builds up to become the hottest portion of the candle, the compounds decompose into hydrogen and carbon. The carbon is what appears as soot on other objects. The outer blue band is where the carbon and hydrogen are burned to form carbon dioxide ($CO_2$) and water ($H_2O$) from the massive supply of oxygen in the air. The darker blue color is created from the oxygen at the base of the wick.

In the case of the copper pot, the copper is made up of cuprous oxide and cupric oxide, and in contact with the flame produces a bluish-green color. Different elements, when heated, produce different colors. Sodium produces yellow, barium green, potassium a soft violet, and calcium an orange.

It helps to know your subject. The more you know, the easier it is to translate it to a canvas.

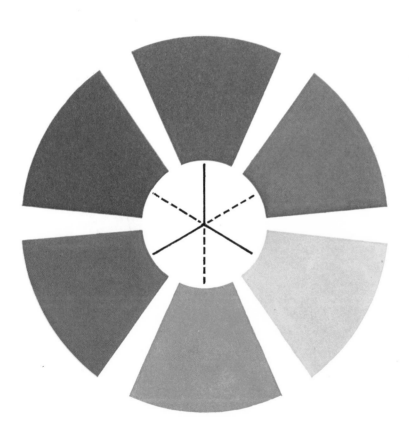

Get accustomed to putting your paint on the palette in the proper order, as described on page 3. The palette is laid out for your convenience, to remind you which colors are hot, warm, cool, and cold.

In putting out the medium that you intend to use (I suggest retouch varnish), fill your cup three-quarters full. This will keep the medium from getting dirty when you dip your brush into it. If your medium is so shallow that the brush touches the bottom, the paint that has settled there will be stirred into the medium, giving it a muddy appearance.

After you have finished painting, let the medium set for a short time, allowing all sediment to settle to the bottom of the container. Then you can pour the medium back into its container, leaving the sediment behind. Wipe out the sediment with a rag, leaving the cup ready for the next time you paint.

## When you have finished painting

Be sure to clean your brushes.

Tear off the used portion of your palette, saving the paint or throwing it away.

Roll up your newspapers and dispose of them.

Return the medium to its container and clean the can.

**Cleaning Up**

### Cleaning your brushes

When cleaning your brushes, first wipe out all the paint you can with a rag.

Using turpentine or any other cleaning agent suitable for removing oil paint, fill a metal cup or can or a glass jar full enough so the brush won't touch the bottom of the container. *(Some people are allergic to turpentine—you will know it very quickly if you are one of them. If so, use something else.)*

Simply dip the very tip of the brush into the turpentine. Capillary action will draw the turpentine into the brush all the way to the metal part. Then wipe the brush again. Repeat this procedure until no more paint comes out of the brush. Straighten out the bristles or hairs to the shape the brush is supposed to be and let it dry. *Do not* wash your brushes with soap and water. If you follow this method, your brushes will be soft and ready for use. (I never ruin a brush as a result of not cleaning it; it just wears down.)

The turpentine can be poured back into the container for reuse, as it is still clean. But be careful with your paint rags. Especially, do not throw them into a place where they might start a fire by spontaneous combustion.

Oil paint is difficult to remove from carpets, furniture, et cetera. To remove oil paint from carpets and clothes, use a liquid soap. Pour it onto the surface touched by the oil paint and let it set for two seconds; then wash it out. (Better still, do not do your painting where there are carpets.)

Some of the colors on the palette are harder to remove than others. The dye colors, such as Prussian Blue, Alizarin Crimson, and Viridian Green, are probably the most difficult. The metallic colors or earth colors (the ones made from different kinds of clays) are the easiest to remove.

I suggest that you spread newspapers down around where you will be painting, whether you are using a table easel or a stand-up easel. This will keep the paint off the floor, because accidents do happen no matter how careful you may be. Suddenly you drop your brush, or you accidentally drop your palette on the floor.

If you do get paint on your clothes, do not use turpentine to clean it off. Turpentine, in contact with your skin, may cause the skin to burn or blister. You may want to put some kind of hand cleaner on your hands before you paint so that if you do get paint on them later on, all you will have to do is wash your hands. This is the best way to start.

It is a very good idea to wear a smock or an old, large shirt over your clothing. You can save yourself a lot of headaches that way. It is easier to keep paint off your clothes than it is to remove it.

**SPECIAL TECHNIQUES**

### Realistic painting

One thing to consider when painting anything—a landscape, seascape, or whatever: Keep in mind that I am speaking of realistic paintings. If you are going to be an abstract artist, then that is a different story, not treated in this book. I am speaking of realism when I instruct you to do this or that. I am speaking in terms of what you must do if you want your picture to look realistic. There are many rules that can be broken, even in the painting of realism, but there are certain basic principles that should be followed. For instance, if you want your water to look wet, there is a certain thing you must do to achieve that effect, instead of its looking like part of the ground or a blank wall standing there. You will discover some of these basic principles as you follow the directions in this book.

### Lighting

Lighting is one of the most important lessons to be learned in painting. The light source—that is, where the light is coming from—should be the lightest part of your painting.

Whether it is midnight, eight in the morning, or late afternoon, the light will always come from the sky, so that should be the lightest part. Now, that does not mean that if you are painting something white you have to paint the sky lighter than the white. I am talking about the light sources. The next darker tone would be the ground. The ground lies at a direct angle to the sky. The next darker area could be a rolling hill or something that is at an angle to the ground, and then the darkest part of the painting would be the uprights, such as tree trunks, telephone poles, et cetera.

Keeping this general information in mind, there are certain basics to follow so far as lighting is concerned. First, you must determine the direction from which the light is coming. For example, your painting could be backlighted, front-lighted, lighted from overhead or from the right or left. Lighting should, however, be consistent throughout the painting.

### Depth perception

There are three ways of achieving depth in your painting:

1. *Linear perspective.* Lines such as of fence posts going back into the distance or a road disappearing into the back-

ground are examples of how the illusion of depth may be achieved, particularly by a beginner who has not learned all the subtleties that might be employed. As a matter of fact, I hate to introduce perspective to beginners, though it is nothing to be afraid of. It is something that can be used with great effectiveness to achieve certain illusions, but for now we will be content with using fence posts and roads and the like.

2. *Aerial perspective.* Colors are also used to achieve the effect of depth in a painting. Warm colors advance or appear to come forward, while cool colors recede. The warmer and darker, the more they come forward; the cooler and lighter, the more they recede. Aerial perspective is very important, but it cannot be achieved by simply adding white to make a color lighter or black to make a color darker. That is why the identity of your colors on the palette as being hot, warm, cool, and cold is so important. Colors must be cooled off or warmed up depending on the effect you are trying to achieve.

3. *Textural perspective.* Painting a surface with a rough or smooth effect will help to create the illusion of depth. For example, it would be foolish to paint your sky area with a rough look and paint the foreground very smooth, because you would not be achieving any textural perspective. You might have a cobblestone road in your painting that goes all the way to the back; while you know that cobblestones are rough in the foreground *and* in the background, you cannot paint them that way. If you did, you would not achieve the perspective you need. Keep in mind that while you know the cobblestones are rough, you would be unable to see the details at that distance, so you paint the cobblestones in the foreground with a rough texture, smoothing them out as they recede into the distance.

## Shadows

One of the most common mistakes that artists make is in painting shadows. Shadows are transparent; you can see details in them. No matter how bright the light or how dark the shadow, you can still see detail in it. For example, if you were to paint a sunset with grass and foliage in the foreground, with maybe a tree or an old windmill, you would not paint them black to indicate shadow, for no matter what time of day, you can still see details in the shadows. Here you have a strong contrast between the light source and your uprights (grass, trees, windmill) silhouetted against the sky, but you must still paint them so you can see the details.

In mentioning these things early, perhaps I can help you avoid some of the mistakes you might make. How do I know in advance what mistakes you are apt to make? I have made them all myself.

In painting shadows there are several things to be considered. First of all, the shadow area is blocked off from the light source; this is what causes the shadows. However, there may be many shadows originating from the same object, and even the same shadow may vary in darkness, from dark to light. All of this is due to the behavior of light, for even though an area may be cut off from the direct rays of the light source, the light reflected from other objects may be diffused into the shadow. The only way you could have an extremely dark shadow would be to have no light source.

The reflection of light follows definite principles, and it might be well to do a little research into the behavior of light, because the more you know about what is going on, the more effective you can be with your painting. But, without being technical, perhaps I can explain a little of what happens.

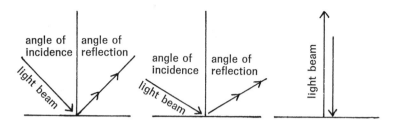

Light from the sun strikes an object and is reflected so that the angle of reflection is equal to the angle of incidence, as shown in the above diagrams.

Light reflected from one surface may strike another and be reflected again, and so on and on. That is the way light may be diffused into the area of the shadow, giving it an effect of translucence and making it possible to see details within the shadow.

In reference to painting, the closer you are to the base of the shadow, the warmer your color is going to be. The far end of the shadow will be cooler, and get warmer as it gets closer to the object casting the shadow. You will be more apt to achieve the effect of shadows by using transparent colors to paint your shadows.

As you start to paint, you will notice things more precisely as you hear about them and are actually doing and applying this knowledge in practice.

## Glazings

Glazings are a very interesting part of painting. A glaze is simply a mixture of a transparent color and a lot of medium, to the consistency of a watercolor. It is a color that you can see through, and is used to go over a dry painting to achieve even more depth. For instance, if you wanted to push your hills farther into the background, you would simply take green, which is a transparent color, and the medium, and paint over the whole painting. The glaze will allow all of the details to show through without changing them or the color except to darken or cool it. This is a very effective technique. If you should want to reverse the effect and pull something closer to you in the foreground, you would use a hot transparent color—Burnt Sienna—with a lot of medium and glaze with that. Try it. It is a lot of fun; but keep in mind that your painting must be dry before applying a glaze.

As you gain experience, you can try other glazes. Burnt Sienna and Ultramarine Blue, both of which are transparent colors, will make even deeper shadows. Put in some deep shadows to see how the colors soften the effect.

## Washes

A wash is transparent too. It is very thin, with a lot of medium, painted onto a blank canvas. For instance, you might be painting a stream of water and want to paint in an undertone of the water; then you would use a transparent wash, going back over with detail later. Washes are also very effective.

If you wanted to paint a white bird, you could use a wash of Viridian Green with a lot of medium to paint in the dark shadow parts, green being a cool color. If you wanted to make the shadow even deeper, you would mix Viridian Green and Alizarin Crimson for a blue-gray color, still transparent, and fill in the darker shadow. In the areas where the sun is hitting, resort to your White, which is an opaque color, and Burnt Sienna for warmth—a tiny touch of Burnt Sienna and a lot of White to fill in just the light areas. This can be very effective, but White is one color that causes a lot of problems—the one that can muddy up the rest. A beginning artist often makes the mistake of using a lot of White in a shadow, perhaps the whole shadow, and discovers that it is a mistake, for White is opaque and shadows are transparent. There are many ways to lighten colors without using White.

## Scumbling

Scumbling is another interesting technique. It must be used on a dry painting. It is a form of highlighting. You can use White or any warm color you want, possibly Yellow or Burnt Sienna, but keep your brush dry, with no medium in it. Then simply drag very lightly over the area you wish to highlight. This catches on the high little ridges of paint and is very effective as a highlight on a bush, for example. It can soften the appearance of the ground or can be used to get a little sheen on the water, as though the wind has blown across it and actually lightened up one particular area of the water. If you use scumbling on the water, use a horizontal stroke.

It can also be used to give a foggy appearance. If you have a painting that is already finished (and dry) and you would like to introduce a foggy condition, then use Viridian Green plus Raw Umber plus White; then very softly go over the painting, letting the brush catch on the high ridges of the canvas.

## Hints to help the beginner

Sometimes accidents happen when you paint. You might accidentally get a touch of red into the sky that you had not intended. Don't panic; the easiest thing to do is to neutralize red. You simply add an opposite color, in this case green. This cools the red, turning it to gray that can easily be wiped off or covered up. To try to wipe the red off would tend to mess up your canvas or tint the other colors with red.

Red, incidentally, is one of the hardest colors on the palette to work with. You cannot add White to lighten it. If you do add White, you get pink. While you can add White to a green and still have green, it doesn't work with red. You lighten red by adding yellow; for highlight, use the opposite color of red—green.

One difficulty you may run into in applying paint to a canvas is getting your paint too thin with medium. Sometimes a beginner will tend to stretch out a little paint by adding more medium and it gets too thin, or try to work with the paint as it comes out of the tube and find it too thick. If it is too thick, it tends to bead up as though it had grains of sand in it. Then the paint is too dry. A little experience will help. Your paint should be neither too thin nor too dry. It should be just right.

One question that arises quite often is: Should one copy a picture? My answer is: I don't see anything wrong with beginners copying a picture unless they try to pass it off as an original idea. It is important for beginners to have a model to go by while they are learning techniques; they will be ready to compose their own quickly enough and will have no desire to be copying another's work.

## Painting a sunset or sunrise

In painting a landscape with a sunset in it, or a sunrise or a moonrise, the arrangement of colors is always the same. A sunrise or sunset follows the order of the spectrum, starting at the horizon line with red and proceeding upward to a red-orange, orange, yellow-orange, yellow, yellow-green, green, blue-green, blue, indigo, and violet. So, depending on where the sun is in relation to the horizon, the colors used will vary in intensity; otherwise, they do not change. For the color of the sun or the moon never changes—it is always the same. Color changes in the sky are due to the refraction of light as it passes through the atmosphere, and the more dense the atmosphere (the more dust particles there are), the brighter the colors. Too, the closer the sun or moon is to the horizon line, the brighter the colors, still due to the refraction of light. Start observing these phenomena more closely, and you will be surprised to see how your increased knowledge shows up in your painting.

## Painting clouds

Clouds create colors in the sky, still due to the behavior of light as it is refracted or reflected. If you were to get up early in the morning and observe the clouds before the sun rose, you would discover that they are just gray. Then, with the first peak of light, as the sun comes up over the horizon, the uppermost part of the cloud will be a soft pink color. As the sun rises a little higher, the pink color will move downward and the upper part will turn to red-orange. Then, as the sun moves even higher, the pink moves down, the red-orange moves down, and the upper part becomes orange. As the sun gets higher still, the red moves on down that part of the cloud closest to the surface of the ground and the colors proceed upward to red-orange, orange, yellow-orange, and so on. The brighter the colors get, the lighter they get. Would you believe that yellow is lighter than white?

If you want to lighten white, you put a little yellow in it. If you want to achieve the illusion of a black that is blacker than black, then you would add a little violet to it.

Make a few tests to see how effective the use of color can be when you are using black. Mix Burnt Umber and Ultramarine Blue to make black. With this mixture, paint a little square on your palette and then add a touch of violet and notice the effect. Then paint another black square, and with a touch of Prussian Blue paint a dot in the middle of the black. This will look as though you have painted a hole right in the middle of the black, because Prussian Blue is such a cold color and black is a warm color.

These are just a few techniques that make painting more interesting, and the more you know about it, the more fun it becomes.

Now, getting back to the clouds, you can use the hints above to get the effects you want. For instance, if the cloud is yellow and you want to paint the shadow side of it, you will add violet, because violet is the opposite color to yellow. The violet will be added to the yellow and painted on the cloud as the cloud shadow.

As you move down to the orange color, use blue to make the shadow, since blue is opposite to orange.

Viridian Green is a useful color to use in a cloud for a reflected light. As light is reflected back and forth between clouds, a reflection may be coming from within a shadow. Viridian Green is a good color to achieve that effect because it is a transparent color.

The hints in this section should help you to avoid some of the mistakes that beginning painters are apt to make, but it will by no means eliminate them all. Observation and practice will take care of the rest.

YOU CAN PAINT THIS PICTURE
*—I Promise!*

Sixty-one step-by-step photographs
demonstrate the evolutionary process of
painting a seascape using a 12″ X 16″
canvas or canvas board.
The author's painting time was forty
minutes. Your painting time will probably
be one and one-half to three hours.
Relax, take your time, and have fun!

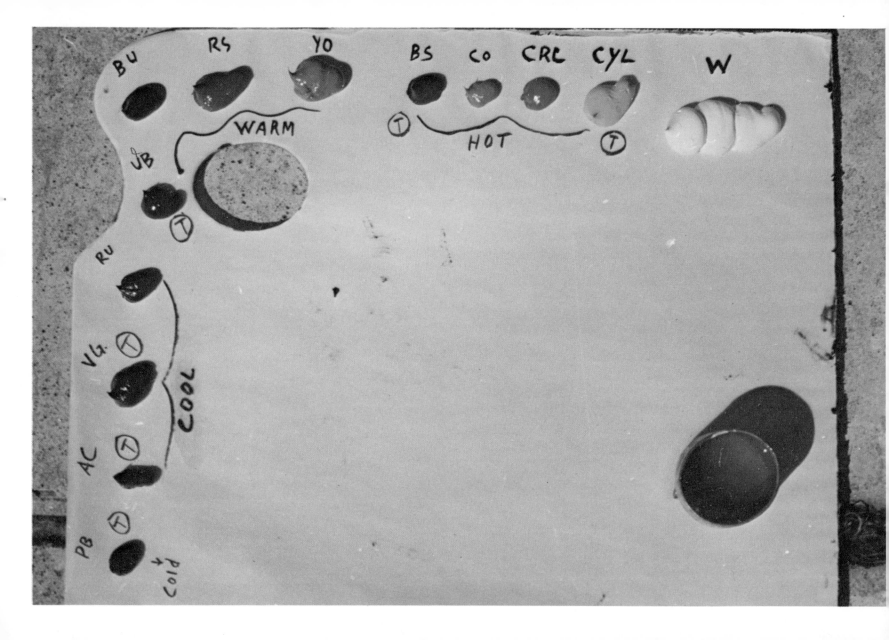

Lay out your palette in the order shown on a 12″ X 16″ disposable palette. Squeeze the paint out close to the edge—the sealed edge would be best, so that if you run out of room you can simply tear away part of the sheet, leaving the paint behind while exposing a clean surface below.

Start with White on the upper right, followed by the four hot colors: Cadmium Yellow Light, Cadmium Red Light, Cadmium Orange,* Burnt Sienna; then the warm colors: Yellow Ochre, Raw Sienna, Burnt Umber, Ultramarine Blue; then the cool colors: Raw Umber, Viridian Green, Alizarin Crimson; and last the cold color, Prussian Blue.

The letter T is used to identify the transparent colors on your palette. There are six: Prussian Blue, Alizarin Crimson, Viridian Green, Ultramarine Blue, Burnt Sienna, and Cadmium Yellow Light.

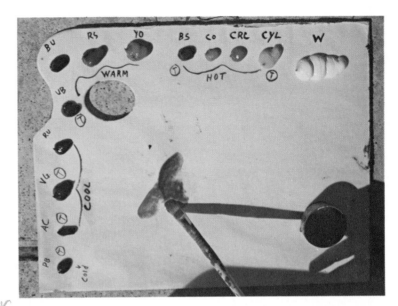

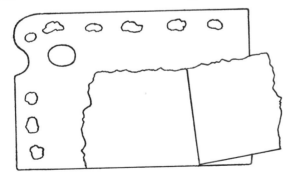

*Be sure to use plain Cadmium Orange without berium.*

Fill an oil cup with retouch varnish (liquid). Dip the #7 bristle brush into the varnish. (If it is a new brush, be sure to flip out all of the plastic coating that was applied to the brush at the factory to protect the shape.) Now pick up a very tiny touch of Viridian Green, which mixed with the varnish should give you a very transparent blue-gray color. *Do not add White,* which would opaque the color.

With this mixture, you are going to do your beginning sketch. Keep the sketch very simple. The reason for using a transparent color to make the sketch is obvious: It is easy to cover it up.

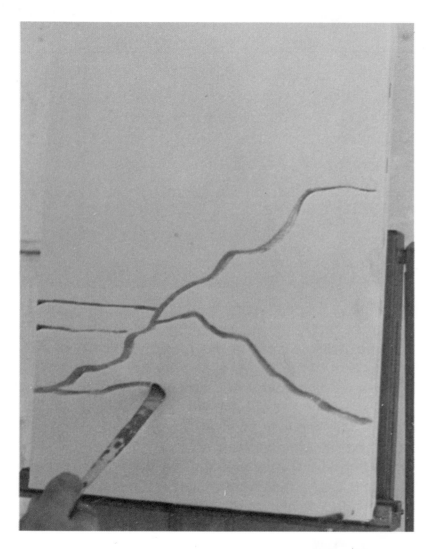

Paint a simple line for the water and the water next to the beach. Add lines outlining the sand dunes. It is not necessary to put in grass or any other details at this point.

*Do not* put the horizon line, which is the same as the eye-level line, in the center of the picture. In this case, the horizon line is where the sky and water meet. Keep the line straight across the canvas.

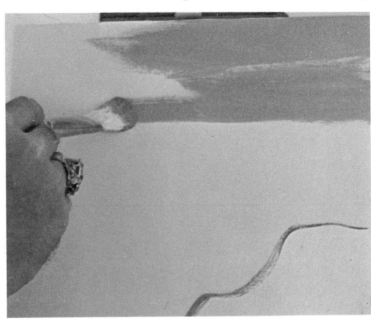

First of all, where you start a painting is very important. In this painting you will start with the sky.

Fill the #12 flat bristle brush full of White and enough retouch varnish to make the paint very creamy. Then, partway into the brush, mix Ultramarine Blue with a tiny touch of Burnt Umber to gray the blue. Let this mixture work up into the brush to about one-third the end of the brush. Mix paint into both sides of the brush by turning the brush over. This mixture is for the upper part of the sky.

Starting at the top of the canvas, paint the strokes straight across and fill up about one-third of the sky area with this color. You will use three different bands of color for the sky; this is the reason for filling only a third with this color.

Now, into the same color on your palette, pick up more White plus a touch of Viridian Green. Mix into the brush so that you have it worked in on both sides of the brush. In that way you can take advantage of back-and-forth brush strokes.

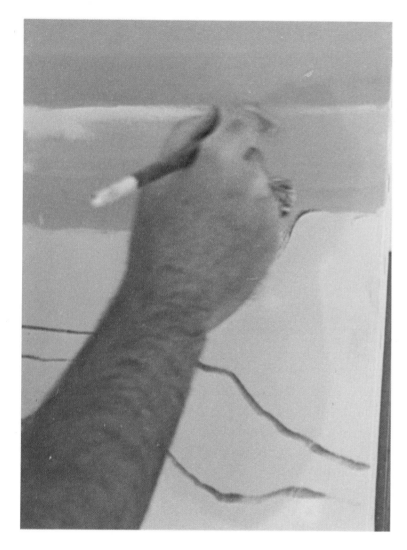

Using the same stroke, paint the lower part of the sky, working up toward the first color you painted in the upper portion of the sky. Blend the two colors as smoothly as possible, trying not to leave a definite line where the two colors meet. This is achieved by painting over both colors at the same time.

Now, lighten the same color by adding more White and a touch of Raw Umber. Keeping the strokes straight across the canvas, start on the horizon line and work up to the other color, again blending the edges where the two colors meet.

Try not to leave harsh lines when color changes occur; in other words, you would not want to be able to take a pencil and draw an outline of where the color change took place.

Now, using the fan brush, which should be held all the way back on the handle, just simply wave your hand. Fan at a 45° angle to help blend the color better. Then fan straight across. Always be sure to end up with strokes straight across.

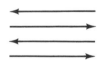

Be sure to end up with strokes going across the canvas.

**Loading Brush to Paint Water**

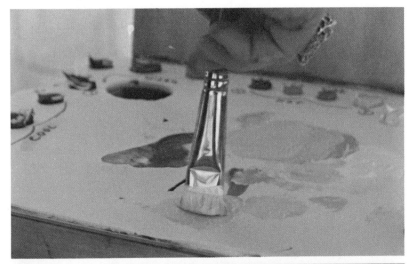

Pick up White plus Viridian Green by holding brush handle straight up, as shown above, pressing down on bristles as you pull the brush toward you. This will build up a ridge of paint along the back side of the brush.

Now add Viridian Green plus a touch of Yellow Ochre to the middle part of the brush and Burnt Umber plus Ultramarine Blue to the end of the brush.

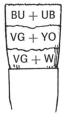

loaded brush

Starting along the horizon line, work from right to left. Hold the brush in as you pull it to the left, lowering the handle to start picking up paint out of the heel of the brush. This technique will give you three bands of color out of your brush in one stroke. The ridge of paint built up on the brush should come off on the canvas in two ridges, which will be the part where the water meets the shore. You may have to go back with a brush stroke straight across to straighten up the horizon line.

**Wet-Sand Stroke for the Beach**

Using Raw Umber added to what you were using, make a stroke across the canvas, pushing up under the ridge of paint to cover the canvas and also to accentuate the water's edge.

Add more White plus a tiny touch of Burnt Umber to warm the color, thereby making the color appear to come closer to you. Pick up a little Raw Umber in the corner of the brush to paint tire tracks. Try to complete each track in one stroke. Start at back and come forward in a semicircle or oval effect and make two lines. The tracks should be closer together at the back toward the horizon line. Now fan straight across the beach.

**Making Waves with the Liner Brush**

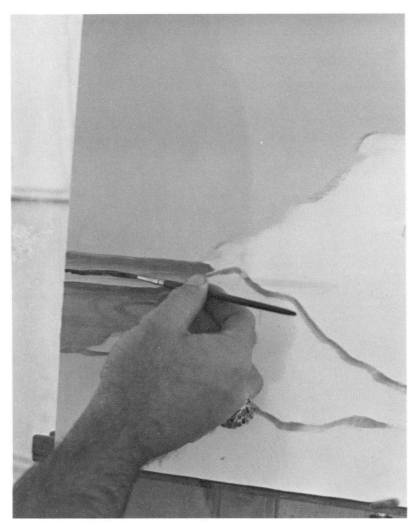

Load the liner brush with lots of varnish to get it very wet. Then pick up Viridian Green plus Raw Umber to make a very dark green.

This is applied by laying the brush flat and pulling it across the canvas in a horizontal stroke. As you pull the brush across, roll it slightly to keep it from getting too flat, and also to keep dark paint coming out of the brush.

Using White plus a tiny touch of Yellow Ochre, smooth the two together slightly, using the painting knife. Then scrape up a small but long line of paint on the palette. Then bounce the knife up and down in the pile of paint to create a sawtooth edge on the knife.

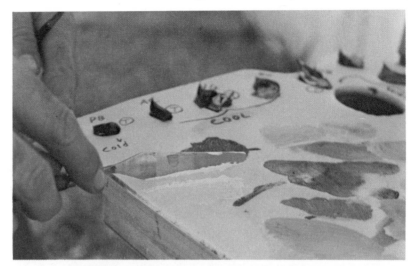

Now, using the edge of the knife, touch the top part of the waves with an in-and-out motion to create the whitecaps.

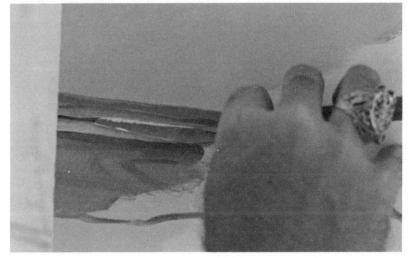

**The Completed Wave**

Don't play with it. Put the paint on and leave it alone. If you should get too large a glob of paint, simply take the fan brush and slice off what you don't want by using a horizontal stroke. You can make another wave behind the front wave, but it should not be as large as the front wave. If it looks good at this point, leave well enough alone. The more you work at it, the more you will tend to eliminate the feeling of what the paint is doing. Tilt the canvas forward to see how the light pattern catches on the raised part of the water. Then, when your painting is on exhibit and the light changes, visitors will say, "Wow!"

In painting the light side of the dunes, load the brush in a clean spot; but still using the #12 brush just as it was, pick up lots of White and a little Burnt Umber.

Apply the paint so as to cover the canvas in as few strokes as possible. Pull the brush to paint in the direction of the hill.

dune

Paint in the direction you want the paint to go.

Add more White and Cadmium Orange to warm the color as you make the sand appear to come toward you. Add Burnt Sienna to make the color darker. As colors get warmer and darker, they appear to come forward the more. Notice how some of the blue works out of the back of the brush. This gives the effect of soft shadows.

Pick up Burnt Umber for the right side of the dunes in back. Then use Ultramarine Blue plus Burnt Umber to make ripples in the sand. This effect can be achieved by taking off and putting on pressure as you pull the brush in one stroke across the canvas. This gives a washboard effect.

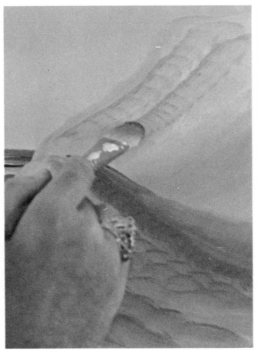

Continue the stroke from the dark into the light side to give the light side some ripples.

Be careful not to overdo the ripples, as it would tend to get monotonous. Some beginners make two strokes that look so great that they make two thousand more just like them. This is when the painting gets boring. It is better to do too little than too much.

After you have painted all the ripples in the sand, use the fan brush to soften. Fan in the direction in which the sand is moving. *Do not* get into the sky or water. Sand is also soft, so the fan stroke will help to create that effect.

At this point, stand back and look at your painting. Not bad! The canvas is now covered, but it appears to lack something, so why not paint some grass to give it life?

A little word of advice. This next step will make you think you have ruined the whole thing, but don't worry. It will turn out beautifully if you will do just as I say. I promise!

*Do not* add varnish.
*Do* use lots of paint.

**Picking Up Paint to Make Grass**

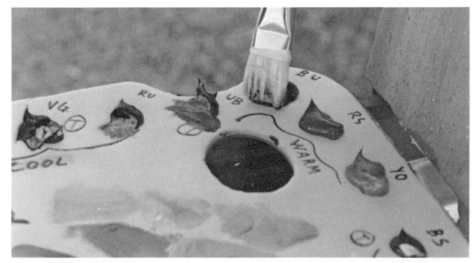

Start with Burnt Umber and dip into the pile of paint and pull the brush toward you. Then repeat with Ultramarine Blue plus Viridian Green plus Alizarin Crimson plus Prussian Blue, as shown below. You can see how the paint is all on one side of the brush.

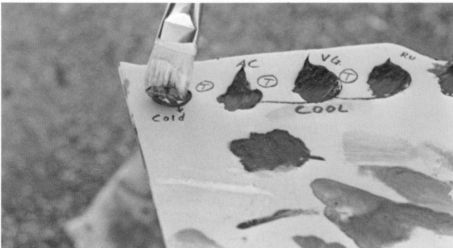

Apply the paint on heavily and in one stroke. What happens is that by picking up the paint in the order I gave you, it is going onto the canvas with the cool side down, which is the way it should be, as the grass will be cooler in the shadow.

Make another stroke following the shape of the sand dune, and then one more in the foreground. Pick up more paint if necessary.

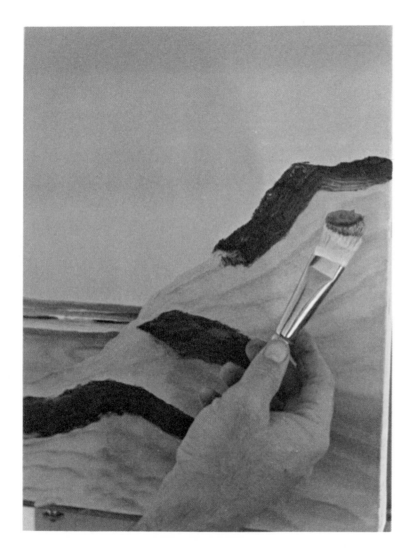

Now pick up Raw Sienna plus Yellow Ochre in the same manner that you used for the dark side. *Do not* clean out the brush.

Apply paint on heavily so color will extend into the sky area and cover into some of the dark part of the grass.

Add Cadmium Yellow Light plus Yellow
Ochre to paint the middle grass, taking what
is left in the brush to paint the grass in
the foreground.

At this point the canvas should look like a total disaster, and you may want to give back the book along with your painting, but let's take another step first. This part will please you, because it is easy to do, is an effective way of creating grass, and will restore your confidence in your ability to paint and my ability to instruct—I hope.

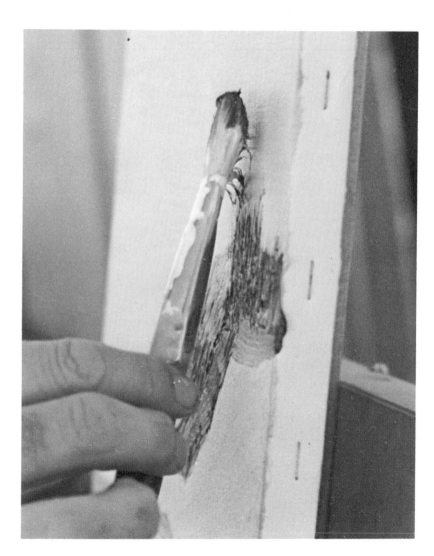

Hold the brush as shown, with the handle close to the canvas. Look at the photograph to see what the brush is actually doing. Just a few of the bristles are doing the work.

Push up lightly on the brush so that only a few bristles are pulling up through the paint. Start in the dark area, pushing up through the light. Do one stroke after another.

You may have a tendency to skip around. *Don't!* Do one stroke so that it slightly overlaps the other. Push straight up.

Let your brush do the work. You just push it. In that way, if it doesn't look right, you can blame it on the brush.

Proceed on down to the next clump of grass and use the same technique. The grass will automatically appear to come forward because of the warm colors you are using.

To finish up the bottom edge, simply go below the line and push up on the brush. If you don't do this, you will end up with a hard line, such as the one above.

Now take the fan brush and drag away from the bottom of the grass very lightly. This technique will create shadows and softness.

Isn't it fun to find out how easy painting can be?

At this stage the picture looks good but still needs some details. You have come this far—why not really "jazz" it up?

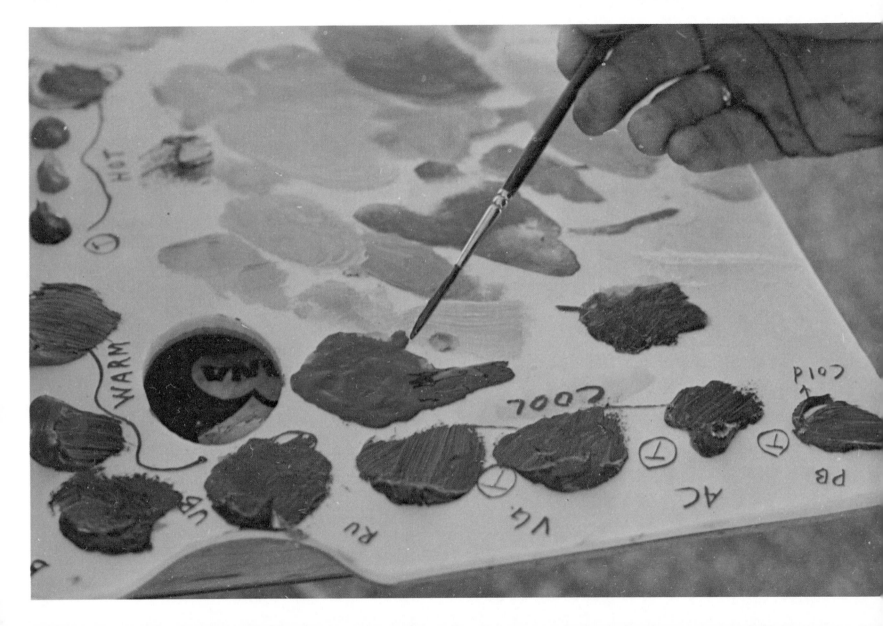

Using the liner brush with lots of varnish (and I do mean lots of varnish), mix Burnt Umber and Ultramarine Blue (my mixture for black) on a clean part of the palette. Be sure the brush is loaded all the way up to the metal part. This will allow the brush to act like a fountain pen. When you make a stroke, it replenishes itself with more paint through capillary action.

Holding the brush straight in, as shown in the picture above, pull the grass stroke up. If the paint skips, the brush is too dry and needs more varnish.

Let the grass basically blow in one direction. However, it is necessary to have some growing in the opposite direction and some coming toward you. Use the dark all over.

Also pull out in the direction of the shadows, individual shadows, and maybe a shadow or two of grass to be put in later all by itself.

Now add Yellow Ochre and start in the foreground, adding several strokes, though not as many as the dark. Work your way into the background; as your brush picks up some of the dark and tones it down, the color will recede.

Adding Cadmium Yellow Light to lighten
the color, make a few more strokes in front
and highlight individual strands of grass.
Use White added to the brush as a lighter
highlight on the grass.
Now, to make a single strand of grass, as
shown, try this technique: Use White plus
Cadmium Yellow Light in the entire brush,
with Burnt Umber and Ultramarine Blue
on only one side. With one stroke you can
paint both the light and shadow sides of
a single blade of grass. Just be sure that
the shadow side corresponds with the rest
of the shadows in the painting.
Do you like that technique? Do it again!

**Top of Sea Oat**

Load brush with Burnt Umber plus Raw Sienna by pulling the brush flat in one direction toward you. Turn the brush over and pull some more. This will flatten the brush so that it looks like a screwdriver.

Apply the paint as though you were going to slice the canvas with the sharp edge of the brush. This gives you a thin line which thickens up as you pull down to tie into the tall grass.

Angle the brush and pat to achieve the little seeds hanging from the oat. Make the stroke larger at the bottom.

Why not do two more smaller ones?

Highlight with Yellow Ochre plus White. Do not use varnish. Let the brush pick up paint as it comes out of the pile of paint. This will give texture.

**Four-Stroke Sea Gull**

Make a sea gull with White plus Viridian Green for the body.

two strokes

Use Burnt Umber plus Ultramarine Blue for wing tips—one stroke for each, starting at end of Viridian Green plus White of bird, and work it out in one stroke on each side.

A dot for the head is all you need. With a little practice you can get the eyes and bill all in one stroke. Add a couple more gulls now that you know how to make them.

**A Body on the Beach**

Using Cadmium Red Light plus Cadmium Orange on one side of the brush, plus Alizarin Crimson on the other side, make the top part of the body with one stroke, the dark side being on the right.

Use Burnt Umber plus Ultramarine Blue for the legs and a dot for the head.

How about *blue* eyes?

Here is a closeup of the fellow. See the pensive look on his face.

**Highlight Grass**

Highlight grass with some Viridian Green plus White. This is a sky-reflected light, not sunlight, so it needs to be cool.

Some yellow flowers can be made by using Cadmium Yellow Light plus White on the end of the brush and making little dots. Use them in the center clump of grass, off to one side of the clump. This will be an eye-catcher. Don't put in too many, but don't put in too few, either; do it just right.

Finer details can be added to the tall grass with a touch of Burnt Umber, Ultramarine Blue, and Viridian Green.

A log can be made all in one stroke using Burnt Umber and Ultramarine Blue on one side of the brush and White plus a touch of Cadmium Orange on the other side. Hold the brush so that the light side is in the left and start pulling up on the brush. As you pull up, if you twist the brush by rolling it in your fingers, it will give you a gnarled look.

Add little branches so you can put a bird in them. I suggest a yellow-bellied sapsucker.

Why not?

Make the bird with Cadmium Yellow plus White all in one stroke. Then make the dark part with Burnt Umber plus Ultramarine Blue.

Please be careful on the very next step. With the spelling, that is!

It will not be Garden, but, whatever it is, use whatever color you want to sign your name. Keep it inconspicuous, so as not to interfere with the painting itself, but not so inconspicuous that it will not be seen. After all, this may be your very first oil painting; but let's hope that it will not be your last.

This lesson will give you an opportunity to paint a land-scape on your own. There will be no pictures for you to follow, only the directions. This will introduce a technique that is handy when you are out in the field without your paints and brushes. Just a pen and paper will do for a start. With that you can provide all the information you will need to return to your easel and paint. You can indicate the com-position, the colors needed, and the brush strokes. So let's start with a very simple sketch.

Use Viridian Green plus Alizarin Crimson (a tiny touch of each) and lots of medium in your #12 flat bristle brush, using retouch varnish as a medium. Sketch in a line for the water and simple lines for trees, ground area, and the reflection of trees in the water. This is all that is needed to complete a sketch, as shown.

Paint the sky first. Fill your brush with White to about the halfway point. Work it into the brush on both sides so that the paint is equally distributed throughout. Add Ultra-marine Blue with a touch of Burnt Umber, and work this into the brush to mix the colors thoroughly and avoid streaking. Now paint this on the upper third of the sky area, using a horizontal stroke. Start at the top edge of the canvas.

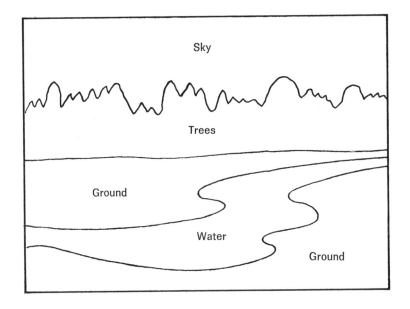

Now add more White and Viridian Green, which will lighten the color and make it cool. Use this to paint the middle third of the sky area, blending in the edges where the colors meet to avoid having a definite line between the two. This is very important. Add more White and a tiny touch of Raw Umber and fill in the rest of the sky down to the tree line. Again, it is necessary to blend the colors so that there is no definitive line to show where the color change took place.

At this point, use the fan brush to soften the color changes even more. Fan the brush at a 45° angle, starting in the lighter area and working up to the dark. Then fan straight across.

Now paint the water. You have the paint left in the brush from painting the sky, which is going to be reflected in the water. An important thing to remember about water is that it reflects what is above it. Water is like a mirror, but water also has color unless it is a crystal-clear lake (of which there are very few). The color of water depends on the sediment which is moving in it. It may have a greenish color from algae or other plants. It may be reddish from red clay washed into it during a heavy rain, or perhaps brown, depending on the earth color present. In the swamp areas of Florida and Alabama, it even appears to be black from the decaying organic matter releasing iron and sulfur into the water. But, regardless of the color, the water still has reflections in it—from the sky, trees, et cetera. However, in this painting you will treat the water as though it is somewhat clear, and your brush strokes are as important as getting the color in the right places.

To make the water appear to be wet, it is necessary to paint using down strokes (straight down), even when there is a curve in the water line. This is what gives it the wet look.

Later you will introduce some cross strokes for another purpose.

Using the last color from the sky, paint the upper third of the water area. Remember that the order of colors here will be the reverse of the order in which they appeared in the sky.

Now add Viridian Green and Ultramarine Blue plus White to paint the middle area of the water (always using a down stroke, of course). These colors may be streaked, as this also has a watery effect. Now add Ultramarine Blue and a tiny touch of Burnt Umber and fill in the rest of the water. Blend the colors where the layers come together so there is no definite line marking each color change.

Next you will paint the reflections of the trees in the water, putting a reflection of the single tree in the foreground. (See the sketch below.) For the background trees use Ultramarine Blue plus Raw Umber plus Viridian Green plus Yellow Ochre and paint the reflections, still using a down stroke, as shown in the sketch. Cover about half of the reflection area—that area closest to the sky reflection. Do not blend the colors very much; the reflection will appear more realistic. Now add Prussian Blue and Raw Umber and paint in the reflection area closest to the ground.

Now pick up Ultramarine Blue plus Burnt Umber on one side of the brush and add White plus a little Cadmium Orange on the other side. With the brush loaded in this fashion, and holding it so the Cadmium Orange and White are on the right side, you can paint the tree-trunk reflection in one stroke. This will give you a dark side on the left and a light side on the right.

Fan the water straight up and down and then across to give the water a surface look. Where the tree trunk is reflected,

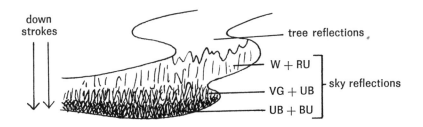

down strokes

tree reflections

W + RU

VG + UB — sky reflections

UB + BU

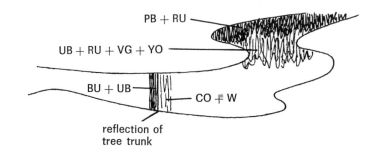

PB + RU

UB + RU + VG + YO

BU + UB

CO + W

reflection of tree trunk

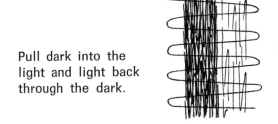

Pull dark into the light and light back through the dark.

turn the fan brush to the side and streak back and forth with a narrow stroke (horizontal stroke) to give movement to the water.

At this point, you will paint the trees in the background. Keep in mind that you will be painting the leaves on the back side of the trees first and those on the front side last. Starting at the top of the trees next to the sky area, use Ultramarine Blue plus Raw Umber plus Viridian Green plus Yellow Ochre. Then, using a scrubbing stroke, put in this color to cover the upper part of the trees. Be sure to let the color extend into the sky area just a little to insure that you are covering the canvas completely. Work in an irregular pattern to make it look more like trees. Now add Prussian Blue plus Raw Umber to paint the bottom portion of the trees.

The next step is to paint in the tree trunks. Fill your liner brush with medium; add Ultramarine Blue and Burnt Umber to make a black; and then, on one side of the brush, pick up a little White, worked in to get a light gray. With the lighter color on one side of the brush, and holding the brush straight in to the canvas, you can paint several tree trunks and branches. Start at the bottom of the tree trunk and paint upward toward the sky. You can make different sizes by pressing down on the brush. Be careful, for you may have the tendency to make them all the same size and the same distance apart. Make several and then be sure to reflect them in the water, using a down stroke. Reflections of images behave the same as the reflection of light. Notice how the reflection of a tree appears in relation to the tree itself.

When you have finished painting the tree trunks, use the fan brush and fan only the water, using a horizontal stroke.

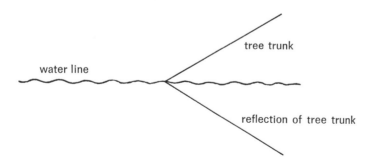

tree trunk

water line

reflection of tree trunk

Now you are ready to highlight with leaves on the front side of the trees. Using the #12 flat bristle brush (no need to clean it), pick up Ultramarine Blue plus Raw Umber mixed together by bouncing the brush into the color. Do this all the way across the brush. Now pick up a little Cadmium Yellow Light and bounce it into the right corner of the brush, and you are ready to paint leaves, letting the light side come off on the right side, as this is where the light is coming from.

Remember that these are leaves in the background and will not have details—just shape and color. You can put a few reflections in the water, but be sure to fan straight across them. Don't overwork it. You might try changing colors a little by adding a little Cadmium Orange or Yellow Ochre on some of the trees.

Next will be the grass, and it is important for you to use lots of paint without medium. Still using the #12 brush (do not clean it), pick up White plus Raw Umber. Do not mix on the palette. Just pick up a blob of White and the Raw Umber on top of it and slide it onto the canvas in the area under the trees. Cover the canvas but do not work over the paint. Try to cover the canvas in one stroke. Now pick up Raw Umber and Raw Sienna and paint the area under the area you have just painted, using the same method. Then add Raw Umber and Ultramarine Blue and paint the area next to the water as part of the background grass. Now, using the same stroke to make blades of grass as was used in "Painting a Seascape," Photo #45, paint the grass blades. Start in the light part and with a soft touch work your way across and down the canvas, letting the darker color extend over some of the light colors.

Make the leaves in patterns like so:

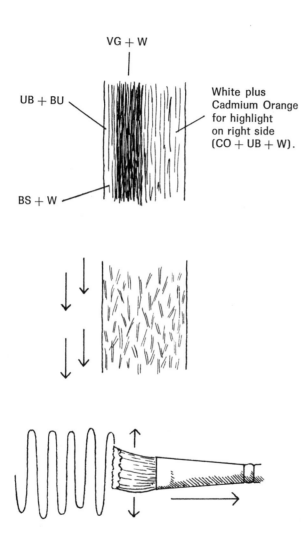

VG + W

UB + BU

White plus
Cadmium Orange
for highlight
on right side
(CO + UB + W).

BS + W

Now you are ready for your tree trunk. This will involve the five values: body tone, body shadow, cast shadow, reflected light, and highlight.

For the cast shadow use Ultramarine Blue plus Burnt Umber; fill the liner brush, using enough medium to make the paint go on easy. This will go on the left side of the trunk, covering about one-fifth of the width. Pull the stroke down; do not paint around the trunk.

For the body tone use Ultramarine Blue plus Cadmium Orange plus White; blending the cast shadow and the body tone will give the body shadow. Use Viridian Green plus White on upper half of the left side for reflected light; Burnt Sienna plus White for the lower half of the left side for warm reflected light.

Now use Ultramarine Blue plus Burnt Umber plus Alizarin Crimson to make the bark effect. This is achieved with short strokes, working dark to light and light to dark in a down stroke. Use an irregular pattern; work into the highlight as well as the reflected light.

For the grass in the foreground, use the #12 brush, filling it with Prussian Blue plus Burnt Umber. Then, in one corner of the brush, add Cadmium Yellow Light. To apply this on the remaining part of the blank canvas in the foreground, you will hold the brush sideways with the Yellow part up and pull the brush across, at the same time moving it up and down.

Now add Cadmium Orange and paint some more. Keep changing the light color, using Yellow Ochre, Raw Sienna, Alizarin Crimson, Cadmium Yellow Light, and Cadmium Orange. Always keep the dark edge of the brush on the bottom and let the colors overlap.

After the canvas is covered, you can highlight the grass by patting the brush, first flat on the palette and then on the tops of the grass. Use light colors like:

Cadmium Yellow Light plus White
White plus Alizarin Crimson
White plus Viridian Green
White plus Cadmium Orange

At this point, you may want to use the liner brush and Ultramarine Blue plus Burnt Umber and lots of medium to sign your name.

Avoid making them all in a straight line, thus:

This.          Not this.

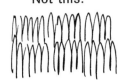

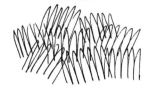

# PAINTING A SNOW-CAPPED MOUNTAIN

This lesson will give you more practice in painting water and introduce you to one of the most difficult colors with which to work—White, used here to give the effect of snow. One of the biggest mistakes a beginner or amateur may make is in using pure White to paint snow. There are many factors to be considered.

First of all, the snow should appear to be cold, but, strangely enough, this is achieved by using warm colors in the light areas and cold colors in the shadow areas. Keep in mind that there are five values in painting a pile of snow, just as there are when painting any other colored object. Snow is similar to water in that it reflects what is around it, though not in the same manner as water. If you were to examine a snowflake, you could understand why. (Do yourself a favor and look at photographs of snowflakes taken under a microscope.) Each snowflake reflects its surroundings, but remember that snowflakes are individual things and are lying at different angles to each other and to their surroundings.

In this lesson, I shall give the instructions in the same way that I would make notes in the field with the intentions of doing the painting in the studio. I shall use initials to abbreviate the names of the colors, symbols for certain notations, and line drawings to indicate details.

Just as a reminder, let's review the palette with this in mind.

White (W) . . . . . . . . . . . . . . . . . . . . . . . . . . . . . . . . .neutral color

Cadmium Yellow Light (CYL)
Cadmium Red Light (CRL)
Cadmium Orange (CO) . . . . . . . . . . . . . . . . .hot colors
Burnt Sienna (BS)

Yellow Ochre (YO)
Raw Sienna (RS)
Burnt Umber (BU) . . . . . . . . . . . . . . . . . . . . . . .warm colors
Ultramarine Blue (UB)

Raw Umber (RU)
Viridian Green (VG) . . . . . . . . . . . . . . . . . . . . . . . .cool colors
Alizarin Crimson (AC)

Prussian Blue (PB) . . . . . . . . . . . . . . . . . . . . . . . . .cold color

**NOTE:** At this point I shall introduce the shorthand notations that I use when I am out in the field without my paints and brushes and see a scene I would like to paint. The rules for these notations are simple, and once you get the hang of it you won't have any problems.

Notice that all the colors on the palette abbreviate so that there are no two with the same initials; therefore, I can use the initials to indicate a color without having to spell it out each time. Now, when I want to indicate a tiny touch (and you by now know that when I say a tiny touch, I mean a tiny touch), I will put a circle around the initials of the color, like so: (BS). For instance, I will make notations for the sky

W + (BS) plus medium to make it work easy, then add an arrow.
↓
VG

The arrow coming down from the first color indicates you should add Viridian Green to the same pile of color you were using before. If the arrow does not come down from the last color, it means you should mix the next color in a clean area on the palette. Arrows will be used also to indicate the direction of the brush strokes. Now, let's try out this notation system on an actual painting.

## Step-by-step instructions

Start with a simple sketch, outlining the component parts of the painting. Using the large #12 brush and a touch of VG plus AC and lots of medium to make a gray color, make a sketch similar to the one shown here.

1. Start with the sky. It is going to be an easy sky to paint, but very effective.

Pick up W + (BS) worked into the White, which will give a pinkish cast. Now bounce this into the sky area, covering the

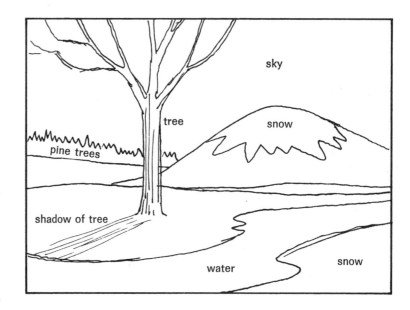

canvas well but leaving some blank areas. You will use three steps in painting the sky, so fill the sky area to about one-third, using strokes at an angle of about 30°.

Now, while you have this color in your brush, use it to paint the water, but use a down stroke.

2. Pick up VG and bounce it onto the sky in the same way as before, filling some of the blank areas left in the sky; also in the water, using a down stroke.

3. Now, use UB + (BS) to fill the remaining areas of the sky. Remember to paint your strokes at the same angle. *Do not* deviate in the direction of your stroke because of the mountain. Add this color to the water, too.

4. With these preliminary instructions, complete the painting by following the shorthand notations provided.

### Sky + sky reflection in water

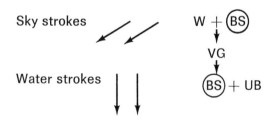

Sky strokes    W + (BS)
       VG
       (BS) + UB

Water strokes

### Mountain

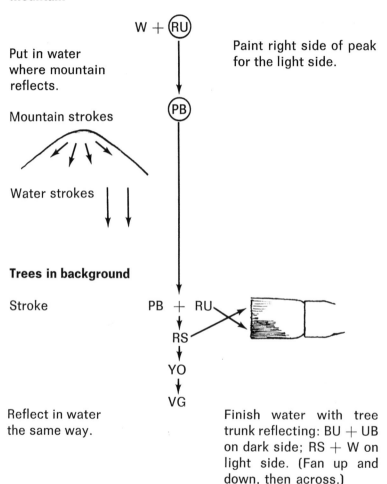

Put in water where mountain reflects.

Mountain strokes

Water strokes

### Trees in background

Stroke

Reflect in water the same way.

W + (RU)

Paint right side of peak for the light side.

(PB)

PB + RU

RS

YO

VG

Finish water with tree trunk reflecting: BU + UB on dark side; RS + W on light side. (Fan up and down, then across.)

## Snow in background

As you come forward to the water, it will be easier to put on all the lights and then come back to paint the shadow side on the left.

W + (RU) light stroke

↓

(PB) for shadow

↓

W + (RS) light

↓

W + (CYL) light

↓

W + (AC) + (PB) + (RS) shadow

W + (AC) + (UB) + (CYL) shadow

At this point, you can use the liner brush to paint lots of trees in the back.

RU + UB + AC + lots of medium

↓

W    on left side

For **ground water** with liner brush to make it move:

stroke

⟶

⟶

W + VG

↓

W + YO

## Large tree trunk

stroke

↓ ↓

BU + UB    cast shadow

↓

BS    body shadow

↓

RS    body tone

↓

YO + W    high light

↓

VG + W

↓

reflected light

BS + W

↓

BU + UB    (bark effect)

**Dead branch** with bird:

BU + UB    dark side

↓

W + CO    light side

**Red bird:** CO + AC + CRL

One stroke for body.

BU + UB back and head

**PAINTING A STILL LIFE**

Canvas size 12" × 16"

A still-life painting involves a few techniques that have not been introduced in the previous lessons. For instance, you will be painting a transparent bottle plus a red apple, both of which present problems, or rather different techniques, but will add to your experience as a painter.

Again, you will start with a sketch. With your #7 brush mix (VG) + (AC) and sketch in the grapes, then the bottle and then the apple with its shadow.

We will use the same shorthand notations as were used in the section on painting a snow-capped mountain. I will indicate brush strokes with arrows, and don't forget that a circle around the color means a tiny touch.

## Background

With #12 brush pick up W + CYL + YO. Starting on the left-hand side of the canvas, paint the background using a down stroke. Don't bend the stroke to go around objects; keep all strokes in a down direction.

Now add RU to the same color you were using to darken the background as you paint toward the right side of the canvas. Add BU to make the top even darker.

## Table

Add CYL to the same color you were using for the background. This will be applied in a horizontal stroke to achieve a flat appearance.

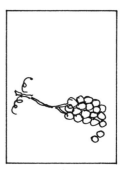

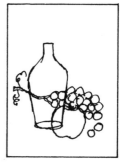

Do not paint over the shadow area but do paint up to it. Do not change the direction of the brush stroke; it should be kept straight across. Add CYL + CO to bring it onto the foreground. At this point the canvas should be covered except for the areas reserved for the grapes, bottle, apple, and shadows.

Now let's review some of the points brought out in previous lessons, particularly the color wheel. While most people have studied the color wheel at one time or another, it will not hurt to review the color wheel as it relates to painting.

The primary colors are red, yellow, and blue. When you mix the primary colors, you get secondary colors. For instance, yellow plus red makes orange; blue plus red makes violet; yellow plus blue makes green. Orange, violet, and green are the secondary colors. When you mix the colors adjacent to each other—that is, a primary color with an adjacent secondary color—you get a triadic color. For instance, yellow plus orange will make yellow-orange; yellow plus green, yellow-green, etc. So the triadic colors are yellow-

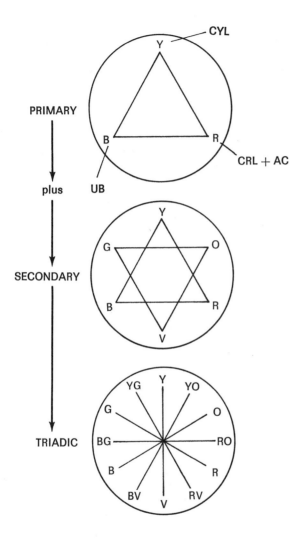

PRIMARY

plus

SECONDARY

TRIADIC

orange, red-orange, red-violet, blue-violet, blue-green, and yellow-green.

One important detail to remember about the color wheel is which colors are directly across from each other—yellow is opposite violet, blue is opposite orange, red is opposite green. You will discover the importance of remembering this as we move to step #3—the shadows.

## Shadows

You were using a yellow-orange on the table, so the shadow must be the color opposite YO, which is BV. In other words, BV must be added to YO to produce the shadow.

Pick up UB + AC to make a blue-violet and add it to the same color you were using, which was CYL + CO. Paint this color straight across the area of the table that appears to be in shadow. Do not pull the brush across the areas reserved for the shadows of the objects. Then fan the background up and down and the table across.

## Grapes

The grapes are to be green. Remember that the light is coming from the right, so everything on the left is going to be in shadow. This step is important if your grapes are to have the proper appearance, and no matter how strange the next step seems to you, it is the correct way to proceed. Block in the grapes in two colors. First, add VG + YO to paint the light side; then mix PB + RU for the dark side. At this point, it is not necessary to make it look like grapes; that step comes next. The painted area should look something like this:

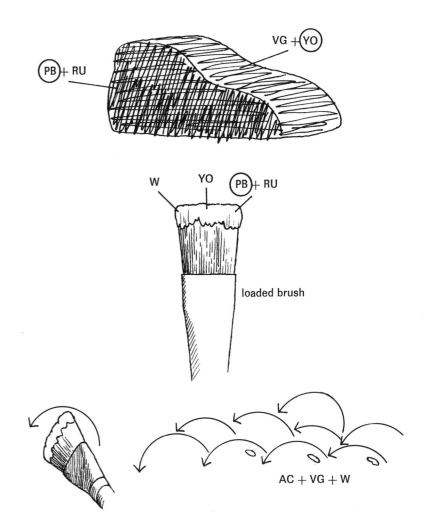

Use the #7 brush to paint the grapes. This step will be very effective if handled correctly. The trick will be in the loading and manipulation of the brush. Pick up (PB) + RU and mix so that the color is green and not blue-green. Then in the lefthand corner of the brush, pick up YO blended into the brush and White blended into the very corner, thus:

Holding the brush with the light toward the top and straight into the canvas (with the handle pointing out), make a semicircle stroke, like so:

Paint one stroke over another. There is no need to refill the brush; just keep moving from back to front and light to dark, making individual grapes. Paint all the grapes and then high-light with a red-violet color: AC + VG + W. Highlight every

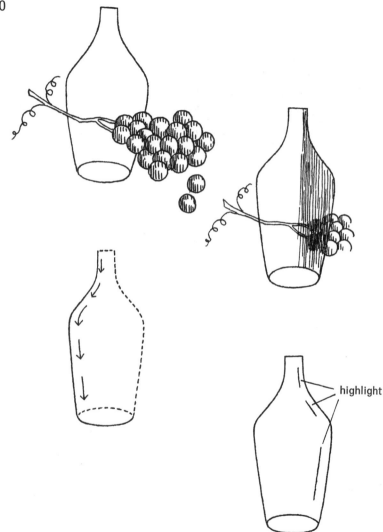

highlight

grape. To make two grapes in front of the rest of the bunch, make these strokes:

Paint the grapes inside the bottle as though the bottle was not even there.

Use the liner brush double-loaded with BU + UB and then pick up W + YO on one side to paint the stem. Highlight with YO on the top edge. Don't pay any attention to the bottle. Paint the stem to reach from the grapes to the other side of the bottle.

## Green Transparent Bottle

Use the #7 brush that has been wiped; no need to clean it completely. Now pick up VG (a transparent color) and paint the bottle as though you were reaching inside to paint the back side. Just work over the stem and grapes, but try to do so in one stroke. The grapes and stem will blur out, but that is the effect to achieve. Now pick up RU + VG and paint the other back side of the bottle and the rest of the bottom. Pick up White, adding it to what is in the brush and a little YO. This will be applied in one stroke down the right side from top to bottom. Then do the same on the left side without picking up more paint.

Use the liner brush to put in some details such as words on the bottom of the bottle. Highlight with a touch of (AC) + W. This is the color opposite to the green and will give a more effective highlight than any other color to be painted on the bottle in one stroke.

## Apple

Clean the brush completely because red is a difficult color with which to work. Paint the apple in the following manner.

Reflected light is achieved by dragging down the left side of the apple, catching background color and apple color at the same time. Use the same technique on the right side. Highlight with (VG) + W.

For the apple stem, use #6 liner brush, adding BU + UB and YO + W to highlight on one side of the brush.

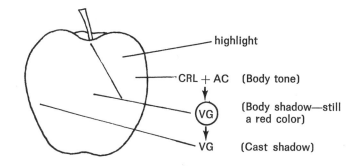

White (W)

Cadmium Yellow Light (CYL)
Cadmium Red Light (CRL)
Cadmium Orange (CO)
Burnt Sienna (BS)

Yellow Ochre (YO)
Raw Sienna (RS)
Burnt Umber (BU)
Ultramarine Blue (UB)

Raw Umber (RU)
Viridian Green (VG)
Alizarin Crimson (AC)

Prussian Blue (PB)

White (W)

Cadmium Yellow Light (CYL)
Cadmium Red Light (CRL)
Cadmium Orange (CO)
Burnt Sienna (BS)

Yellow Ochre (YO)
Raw Sienna (RS)
Burnt Umber (BU)
Ultramarine Blue (UB)

Raw Umber (RU)
Viridian Green (VG)
Alizarin Crimson (AC)

Prussian Blue (PB)

White (W)

Cadmium Yellow Light (CYL)
Cadmium Red Light (CRL)
Cadmium Orange (CO)
Burnt Sienna (BS)

Yellow Ochre (YO)
Raw Sienna (RS)
Burnt Umber (BU)
Ultramarine Blue (UB)

Raw Umber (RU)
Viridian Green (VG)
Alizarin Crimson (AC)

Prussian Blue (PB)

Book design by Liz Green